CHIL Grieve, Too

Helping Children Cope With Grief

By Joy and Dr. Marvin Johnson

Cover illustration by Ron Boldt

Library of Congress Cataloging-in-Publication Data

Johnson, Joy. Children grieve, too: a book for families who have experienced a death / by Joy and Marvin Johnson.

p. 16 cm. ISBN 1-56123-106-1

[1. Children and death. 2. Teenagers and death. 3. Bereavement in children. 4. Bereavement in adolescence. 5. Grief in children. 6. Grief in adolescence. 7. Child rearing.] I. Johnson, Marvin.

II. Title.

BF723.D3J64 1998

155.9'37'083—dc21

www.centering.org

PO Box 4600
Omaha NE 68104
Ph: 866-218-0101
Fax: 402-553-0507
EMail: centeringcorp@aol.com

Children Grieve, Too

Who among us
would not protect another,
particularly a child,
from hurt and sorrow?

When Lynn and Jessica's mother died, they carefully placed her favorite coffee mug in her hand as she lay in her casket.

Rachael took her grandfather's cowboy boots from his closet, set them beside his casket and wore his Stetson hat during his memorial service.

Judy and Claire were older. They looked at their mother in her casket then looked at each other. They smiled and nodded. Then they drove to her home, went through her jewelry box and returned to the funeral home where they changed her earrings to gaudy pink ones and put her favorite bright pink lipstick on her lips. Judy fluffed up her carefully done hair and Claire painted her fingernails in a color called Pink Glory.

All these children, whose ages ranged from seven to twenty-seven, were grieving and all were taking part in the rituals that make death and remembering mean something to us.

We are often asked:
At what age should a child attend a funeral?
Our answer is: *As soon as a child is born.*

Grief and mourning are love's sorrow.
We think a family who loves together grieves together.
We do not have a choice - we will grieve.
Our choice is *how* we grieve.
Our choice is *how* we teach our children to grieve.

How they grieve their first loss will be part of *every* grief they know for the rest of their lives.

1

What You Need to Know

As a parent or other person who loves a child, guiding children through grief can be frightening. There is a need to:
    protect the child,
    make things better,
    take away the hurt.

You can't do all those things.
But you can be a guide and a teacher. You can tell your child it's all right to cry, that feeling sad is okay and that it's also all right to play. You can say you will be there or another adult will be there to answer questions. You can explain funerals and memorial services, and believe it or not, you can be a very good and effective death educator.

To do that you will need to:
    be honest,
    admit you don't know all the answers,
    listen,
    find some helpful resources,
    be creative,
    and at times, you will need to have courage.

There are still many people who think children should not be told the truth.

There are still many people who do not want children at funerals, wakes or memorial services.

And there are still many people who do not want to believe that children grieve, too.

Remember, these people will not be the ones who later have to explain to your child why she was denied the opportunity to be part of her family during a very important and life-changing time.

The first thing you need to know is how children of different ages react to loss. You don't need to read through every age group. Just find those paragraphs that fit your child's age and concentrate on them.

Infants

While babies obviously don't have language skills and can't think about or realize what is happening, they do respond to the grief of those around them. With any loss, especially that of a parent, the baby responds to the change in schedule, tension in those loving her and the disruption in routine.

WHAT YOU CAN DO:
Keep to the baby's schedule as much as possible.
Keep Baby in her own home with as few people as possible caring for the infant.
Do some extra cuddling.
Talk to the infant as you hold him. While he may not understand, it may help you.

Keisha was three months old when my mother, her grandmother, died very suddenly. I was extremely sad over the death of my mom and Keisha seemed to sense that. She began waking every two hours. She cried at least twice as much as normal. I began wearing a cloth diaper on my shoulder because she spit up so much. Finally, I rocked her when she woke and talked to her about her grandmother. I sang sad songs and cried, snuggling my head into Keisha's blanket. Gradually, things became normal again. She sensed I was sad and someday I plan to tell her that even as a baby, we loved each other through grief, just as we love each other in happy times.

Age Appropriate Responses

Each child, like each adult, grieves differently and according to her own personality. However, children do have behavioral stages where some grief reactions may be common. Knowing these occur, can help us support and care for the children.

INFANTS

-More crying
-Thumb or finger sucking
-Senses anxiety, sorrow

1 YEAR – 2 YEAR

-May cling
-Doesn't want parent to leave
-May sleep more
-May wake frequently
-May be more "hyper"

3 YEAR – 5 YEAR

-Bedwetting is common
-Unable to verbalize feelings
-May ask questions
-Plays "death"
-Reverts to baby talk
-May want bottle and diapers

6 YEAR – 10 YEAR

-Plays "death" and "funeral"
-Shyness may increase
-Acting out may increase
-Grades may suffer
-School may become safe haven

11 YEAR – TEENS

-Anger is normal
-Feelings of "unfaired against"
-Acting out occurs
-Philosophical talk with friends
-Search for spirituality
-Risky behavior not uncommon

Toddlers – Ages Two to Five

Here is the delightful age of first language, first adventures and very little idea of permanence. Two to Five asks, *When is Daddy coming back?* They tend to become babies again, returning to a time when things were safer. Bedwetting, clinging, whining and even having more illnesses are common. *Children*, as Tony Sims says, *are not linear. They're random access. They will grieve, then play, grieve, then play.* They're just beginning to develop understanding.They need to know they are an important part of the family, will always be cared for and can be trusted. Children this age often believe that if they have "bad" thoughts bad things can happen. *If I had just been good, Mommy wouldn't have died.*

WHAT YOU CAN DO:

Be honest. Tell the child why the person died.
Use words such as *dead* and *died.*
Avoid *passed away, gone to heaven, is asleep.*
Answer questions, knowing the questions may not come right away.
Explain what death is (see page 10).
Explain the feelings they may have. Let them know that:
    It's okay to cry and be sad. Even big people will cry.
    It's okay to play, too.
Be sure the child knows that he did not cause the death.
Involve the child as much as possible in funeral planning.
Let her know someone will be there for her during the funeral and in the days ahead to give comfort and support.

Lana was four when her mother died and she became very clingy. She didn't want to go to preschool or be without me, so I always left something of mine with her. . .a set of keys, a purse I filled with the usual things, my sweater. She seemed to know that I would come back for my things as well as for her. It seemed to really help.

Six to Nine

They may know death is final, but they may not want to admit it. Six to Nine has watched cartoons. They've seen violence on television and sometimes in their own lives. They know what it's like to be afraid. However, they may still overestimate their own power to cause the death and may think death is contagious. *If I play with Nancy now that her mother's died, my mother may die, too.* They don't know what to say or what to do. In some ways, when someone we love dies, we adults become a lot like Six to Nines.

WHAT YOU CAN DO:
Ask what the child understands already.
Work from his questions.
Be honest. Use words such as *dead* and *died*.
Explain what death is (see page 10).
Answer questions.
Explain what feelings may come, and that other Six to Nines have similar feelings.
Be sure he knows that nothing he thought or did caused it.
Talk about any fears she has.
Involve the child as much as possible in funeral planning, letting her know what will happen and when.

Jose seemed to grow up after his father died. I told him he was not the man in the family; it was his job to be a little kid, but he just seemed more mature. He did start sleeping with a night light on, and he drew pictures of cemeteries and caskets. He said this reminded him of his dad. I put his dad's things in a "Daddy Box" and gave it to the children. Jose took a bottle of after-shave from that box and kept it in his room. He would smell it every morning. He said it helped him remember his daddy.

We all need more attention and human contact when someone dies. Six to Nine marks the beginning of the end for sitting on laps, being cuddled and hugged and crawling into bed with a parent when things get scary. Cuddle. Hug. Tell him you love him and you'll still be a family, no matter what.

Ten to Twelve

The "Tweens" they're sometimes called. Children this age are in that fragile area between small child and adolescent youth. Friends are very important to Ten to Twelve, and they often believe that grieving will make them seem *different*. They want to be independent but know that they can't yet make it on their own. They may fear abandonment, death of others and their own deaths. They worry about relationships: *Who will care for Grandma now? Who will provide the money we need?* They may seem withdrawn and distant, then very close and vulnerable.

WHAT YOU CAN DO:
Be honest. Give as many details of the death as the child needs and wants. They are usually curious and interested. While Seven may be satisfied that Grandpa's heart stopped working, Twelve wants to know what happened to the heart, how Grandpa was cared for and what will happen to Grandma.

Answer questions.

Explain what feelings may come.

Provide a journal for writing down feelings, thoughts and letters to the person who died.

Offer your love, understanding and support.

Involve the child as much as possible in planning the service.

It was a good six months before Steve would talk about his sister. Her death was sudden, and it just seemed to shut him up. He didn't cry and he seemed very afraid all the time. Finally I sat down and told him I needed to talk. I said how we were still a family, we would be there for each other and it might help if he cried. If he couldn't cry with us, at least try crying in the shower. I said how we loved him just as much as we loved his sister and we'd always remember Jenny, even though we'd be sad a long, long time. All at once he said, "Remember when Jen walked backwards to get the dog to drink from the lake and slipped and fell in the mud?" We laughed and then we began a "Remember When" session. In the coming weeks I also noticed he was taking longer showers.

Teens

Teenage years themselves are a grief experience. It's the loss of a childhood - no more cuddling into laps, getting read to or played with. It's not yet the reaching of adulthood when you can make your own decisions and live your own life. It can be a very difficult time for everyone. *You have to approach a teenager in grief as you would a deer,* Sharon Turnbull says, *slowly, carefully, gently.* Teens may feel guilty because at this time of crisis they're starting to pull away from the family. They may feel scared and actually challenge death, something that is even more frightening to parents who have already buried one child. Boys may become very macho and refuse to cry or admit they have feelings, while girls may count heavily on their friends to listen to them and be supportive.

WHAT YOU CAN DO:
Be honest.
Tell about the death and give details.
Explain what feelings may come.
Encourage him to talk to a teacher, coach or favorite relative if he can't open up and talk to you.
Say what you feel.
Say what you need.
If you need your teen to be especially careful now, explain that you're afraid, too, and it will take awhile to get back to normal.
Touch, pat and hug. Give your love and understanding.
Say it's okay to cry and it's okay for you to cry, too.
Tell her how much you appreciate her.
Respect your teen's need for private time.

When Lonnie was murdered I was scared out of my wits for PJ. She was with a group of friends I didn't really know. She could easily have been killed herself and she seemed so angry all the time. One night I asked if she wanted a hug and she said, "No!" I turned and started up the stairs and she called after me, "Mom, do YOU want a hug?" You bet I did!

What You Can Do

INFANTS

-Keep to baby's schedule
-Keep baby in her own home with few visitors
-Talk to infant as you hold them

TODDLERS

-Be honest
-Answer questions
-Explain what death is
-Explain some feelings they may have
-Remind them they did not cause the death
-Involve them in the funeral
-Let them know they will be taken care of

SIX TO NINE

-Answer questions
-Be honest
-Explain feelings
-Talk about fears
-Involve the child in the funeral

TEN TO TWELVE

-Be honest
-Answer questions
-Explain feelings
-Provide a journal
-Offer love, understanding and support
-Involve them in the funeral service

TEENS

-Talk openly about feelings
-Encourage teen to talk to teacher
  or school counselor
-Encourage them to journal or draw
-Create rituals of memory
-Tell them what you need
-Let them tell you what they need

Death is . . .

Something that can be explained clearly and gently to any child.
And no one can do it better than you.
Older children will have questions about details.
Younger children need a simple explanation.
Sharing your family's religious beliefs is helpful, too.
You may want to start out like this:

When people die, all their body parts stop working.
They don't feel or think anymore.
They don't hurt. They don't breathe in and out.
They don't eat anymore, and they don't go to the bathroom.
They are not sad or scared or happy. They are dead.

Dead is not at all like sleeping.
When you sleep, all your parts work.
You dream and you wake up in the morning.
A dead person never wakes up.
The dead person's body will feel different, too.
The body will be cool and solid.
It will feel a lot like the cover of this book.
After you see the body you may have more questions.
I'll be there to help answer those questions.

The part of the person that laughed and lived is gone now.
What is left is just the body,
    like a schoolhouse without any children,
    like a peanut shell without the peanut.

Everything that lives must die at some time.
Leaves die in Autumn and fall from the trees.
Animals live awhile and then die.
Usually people live a long, long time.
Sometimes accidents happen and people die very suddenly.

However someone dies, we care for that person's body.
The part that was alive may be gone, but the body is still here,
    and is very, very important.

10

Explaining the Funeral

There is nothing a funeral director does that cannot be lovingly and gently explained to a child.
Janice Roberts, **Thank You for Coming to Say Goodbye**

No child should be forced to attend a funeral, any more than she should be forced to attend a wedding, baptism, bar or bah mitzvah or other ceremony marking passages in life.

But children can be encouraged to attend and participate.
Sara didn't want to go to her brother's funeral, but we felt it was very important. I told her that families that love together grieve together, and it was her chance to say goodbye. She was afraid people would see her cry, and we assured her they were going to see us cry, too. It was important that we cry together.

BEFORE YOU TAKE YOUR CHILD TO THE FUNERAL HOME, TELL HER WHAT A FUNERAL IS.
You may want to say: A funeral is when people come together to say *goodbye* and *thank you* to the person who died. Even though that person is no longer here, the body is here, and saying goodbye makes us feel better. It's like watching the end of a movie. You feel finished. We'll still be sad for a long time, but there will be people there who love us and care for us, who will tell stories about our person and who will help us. Someone will talk about the dead person, and there will be some music.

DESCRIBE WHAT THEY WILL SEE.
Open casket: Grandpa is lying in a beautiful box. He looks very still and doesn't move. He is dead, and that is very different than sleeping. Grandpa is wearing his grey suit and the tie you gave him. His glasses are on, too. The inside of his casket is a very pretty light blue, and there are a lot of flowers all around him. He is in a room that has very soft music and lots of chairs.

Be as detailed as you like. Ask if the child has any questions.
If you have a closed casket or it is your custom not to view the body, explain in detail just what the child will see and also what the person would look like inside the casket.

Wakes and Visitations

This is a time when people who loved our person and love us come together to be with us.
This is what you will see. . .
   (describe where the visitation or wake will be).
This is what we will do. . .
   (say what will happen).
People will. . .
   (explain what people will do).

Tell the child that some people will cry and it's okay if you cry or he cries. Sometimes people will laugh, too, because just as we are sad now, we're happy to see people who love us and happiness and sadness can come at the same time.

SHIVA
If you are Jewish, you can say how Grandpa will be dressed in white and wearing his talis. You can explain how your family will sit shiva and burn a candle to remember Grandpa.

CREMATION
You may want to explain that the body is put into a small, special room where there is a special fire. It is not like any fire you have in a fireplace. The special fire turns the body into a soft ash which will go into a beautiful jar called an urn. The urn may be one we pick out as a family.

If possible, meet with someone from the funeral home for a children's visitation and question and answer time.

If your child absolutely will not or can not attend the service, make sure he is somewhere safe where people will not tell him he should be at the funeral. Take pictures of the body and ask about video-taping the service for later viewing, and let the child know the video is available when he wants to see it. Say what happened and who was there.

What Your Child Can Do

There are ways to make the funeral special to the child.
In addition to their own visitation they can:
Draw pictures to put into the casket. They can use plain paper or white paper plates.

Write poems and letters to their person. These can be put into the casket, too.

Choose to put something personal into the casket. Help select the casket and clothes the person wears, especially if the person is very close to them.

Help choose the music.

Write something to be read at the service.

When my mother died, we got 60 carnations instead of a casket floral spray. At the end of the service, her two granddaughters passed a carnation to each person attending.

The children can also give each person a piece of paper upon which they can write a memory or story of the dead person. After the service the children can design a cover and make a memory book for the family.

Your Grieving Child

There are several things which will affect your child's feelings after someone has died. One of the most important is:

YOUR CHILD'S RELATIONSHIP TO THAT PERSON.

In his book, *How Do We Tell The Children*, Dan Schafer tells of a grandfather and grandson who were best buddies. *You could set your watch by them walking down the street*, Dan says. This little boy had deep and long grief after Grandpa died. Earl Grollman, who wrote *Talking About Death*, tells of a different reaction when he talked with a little boy whose grandfather died. *It must make you sad when your Grandpa dies*, Earl said. *I don't know*, the boy replied. *I only met him twice and both times he had bad breath.*

If it's Mom or Dad, Sister or Brother or other special person who died, the child will feel strongly. You can probably expect: regression - going back to ways of earlier childhood such as bedwetting, snuggling with a teddy bear, thumb sucking, crying and sighing, outbursts of anger, pretending the death didn't happen, death and funeral play, playing harder and longer, a drop in grades, aches and pains and sickness or new fears.

In other words, a lot of different behavior is not all that uncommon. Just as we grown-ups grieve with our bodies, our emotions and our spirits, children grieve that way, too.

Let them know you are there for hugs and to answer what you can. Let them know their hugs help you, too. Children need to feel they are doing *something* to help, and hugs are often a child's true specialty.

Remember that you don't have to have all the answers. Your funeral director and your clergy person can be helpful. There are support groups and centers for grieving children and there are many, many resources. This is an important and valuable time for your family. How you guide your child through this grief can make her and his life rich and full.

You are still the greatest resource of all.

ABOUT THE AUTHORS

Joy and Dr. Marvin Johnson are the co-founders of Centering Corporation, the nation's oldest bereavement resource center. Since 1977 they have written and published books for grieving children and adults and presented workshops for families and caregivers throughout the US and Canada.

Centering Corporation is located in Omaha, Nebraska, and today the Centering Family includes daughters Janet Sieff and son-in-law, Ben Sieff.

RESOURCES YOU WILL FIND VALUABLE

Ragtail Remembers by Liz Duckworthy. A story that helps children understand feelings of grief. Good for the death of any loved one.

Thank You for Coming to Say Goodbye by Janice Roberts and Joy Johnson. An actual funeral home orientation with sections for parents, teachers and others.

The Grieving Child by Helen Fitzgerald. One of the basic books in supporting children.

Tell Me, Papa by Joy and Marv Johnson. A gentle explanation for children about death and the funeral.

Children Grieve, Too Video. Several authors of grief books for children talk about what children need and what adults need to know.

When Someone Dies by Sharon Greenlee. One of the most beautiful books for children of all ages.

Lucy Lettuce by Patrick Loring and Joy Johnson. A story demonstrating grief and loss.

A Child Remembers by Enid Traisman. A memory book for children ages 8-12.

Fire In My Heart, Ice In My Veins by Enid Traisman. A journal for teenagers experiencing a death.

When Death Walks In by Mark Scrivani. Information for teenagers experiencing a death.

The Snowman by Robin Helene Vogel. For children who have a parent die.

The Brightest Star by Kathleen Maresh Hemery. For children who have a parent die.

Lost and Found by Ellen Yeoman. For sibling grief.

Since My Brother Died; Desde Que Murio Mi Hermano by Marisol Muñoz-Kiehne.

Sweet Memories by Elaine Stillwell. Healing activities for children and adults.

The Garden Angel by Jan Czech. For death of a grandparent,

The Christmas Cactus by Elizabeth Wrenn. For death of a grandparent.

Lilacs for Grandma by Margene Hucek. For death of a grandparent.

www.centering.org

Special thanks to Centering Consultants: Janice Roberts, Jacque Bell and Louise Vance